ABOUT *IN THIS HOUSE* BY LORETTA DIANE WALKER.

Loretta Diane Walker's house of poems is majestic and delicate at once — immense in depth of vision and perception and tenderly sensitive in all the ways human beings need a house to be — with places to sit and remember, to treasure, and to tend. Her vibrantly descriptive poems honor the hardest days and rooms of being and believe in the beams of light coming back to us, once again, through the windows. They are poems as rich and wise as a profoundly conscious life.

—Naomi Shihab Nye

The deftly-written poems of *In This House* sing of life and loss, of illness and the courage to survive. Loretta Diane Walker's poems inhabit the world of the body in struggle with diabetes and cancer with both honesty and tenderness, just as they do the world of the heart. To borrow a line from the poem, "Barbara," these poems "blast beauty into the long chorus of night."

—Cindy Huyser, poet and editor, author of *Burning Number Five: Power Plant Poems*

In these remarkable poems, Walker writes not only of courage in the face of adversity but also of motherhood, family, gender, race, the bounty of the natural world, and the nourishment art provides to the hunger of the human soul. Her talent as a musician infuses her lines with a haunting musicality which complements her mastery of image and diction.

Walker's poems glow on the page like candles in the darkness.

—Larry D. Thomas, Member, Texas Institute of Letters, 2008 Texas Poet Laureate

Loretta Walker shuttles through the curls of emotions in her powerful book of poetry, *In This House*. Describing her mother's decline through diabetes, the delicate state of siblings comes through poems such as "In the Waiting Room". *Mama was rolled in with two legs;/ she will be rolled out with one./ We are waiting/ to see who can hold back tears the longest.* There is story here. Story of strength and stamina. *I will give you an orange dress, Mama./ It is the only color brave enough to carry your darkness/ in its pocket.* We are touched by her portrayal of her nephew's broken heart in "Shrine of Hormones" *Because I love you more than the day you were born,/ I will not tell you she is just the beginning.* Her lines are clever, moving; words that linger long after the poem, such as in "Jack" *Jack Daniel's been feasting on liver,/ without onions, since before the depression.* Walker is a poet on the rise, her words like a mantra to all who read, such as in "How to Fight Like a Girl" *You must learn to walk/ through the day with a fish of fear/ floating through/ the coral of your belly.* Read this book. Keep it in your nightstand. You will reach for it again and again.

—Karla K. Morton, *2010 Texas Poet Laureate*

Loretta's emails always close with the postscript "Life is a poem waiting to be written." And, oh, what a life hers has been: providing many generations of young children with the music education (and love) they crave and deserve, creating and sharing her own amazing poetry, standing up against injustice and prejudice, and supporting her family, friends, and even herself through horrific health challenges! In life and in this remarkable volume of poetry, Loretta dares not "run from love, power, time or magic." Instead, she "stand(s) in the middle of the palace/ allow(ing) midnight to chime in her/ soiled clothes, rough hands, and combat boots." Every page *In This House* is a revelation, waiting for us to discover and savor.

—Barbara Saxton, Author of *Dual Exposure*, retired middle and high school English Teacher

IN THIS HOUSE

LORETTA DIANE WALKER

BLUE LIGHT PRESS ◆ 1ST WORLD PUBLISHING

SAN FRANCISCO ◆ FAIRFIELD ◆ DELHI

In This House

1st World Library
PO Box 2211
Fairfield, IA 52556
www.1stworldpublishing.com

Blue Light Press
www.bluelightpress.com
Email: bluelightpress@aol.com

Book & Cover Design, Illustrations
Melanie Gendron
www.melaniegendron.com

Author Photo
Chris Walker of Walker's Photography
walker9136@sbcglobal.net

First Edition

Library of Congress Control Number: 2015957681

ISBN 9781421837451

IN THIS HOUSE

CONTENTS

I MAMA'S HOUSE

II PORTRAITS

III IN OTHER PEOPLE'S KITCHENS

IV THROUGH THE SEASONS

V SCARRED TEMPLE

VI SHUTTING THE DOOR

ACKNOWLEDGMENTS

Many thanks to the editors of the following journals in which these poems appeared.

94 Creations: "Methuselah," "Sisters," "To a Broke Poet," "How to Fight like a Girl," "A Letter to the Woman in a Black Dress Standing near the Window."

A Book of the Year, Poetry Society of Texas: "Watering the Garden," "Mama's Hands," "Of Dead Begonias," "Bandana Sunday," "Leaving Bob."

2015 AIPF Di-Verse-City Anthology: "In This House."

Boundless 2014: The Anthology of the Rio Grande Valley International Poetry Festival: "Joy on the Heel of Brokenness," "A Sudden Darkness," "Seeking Smooth Air."

Concho River Review: "Liquid Fist."

Connecticut River Review: "Visitation."

Elementary My Dears Anthology: "Flood"

Encore Prize Poems: NFSPS: "Renegotiation."

A Galaxy of Verse: "Monday Mammogram: A Conversation with Karla K," "Stuck In the Gray, "When the Heart has Wings," "Barbara," "The Way He Sees Her," "Diagnosis," "Carol."

Haight-Ashbury Literary Journal: "Vignettes on Love."

Harp-String Poetry Journal: "The Cold Arm of June," "Early Morning Symphony," "Dried Milk," "Cold Cornbread."

Her Texas: "The Help's Daughter," "How to Fight like a Girl,"

Kind of a Hurricane Press: "Watching from the Chair by the Window."

Illya's Honey: "Do Not Disturb a Poem," "From the Diary of Queen Vashti: A Letter to Esther," "The Help's Daughter," "Spring Thirst," "When the Earth Writes Poetry," "The Scream," "September Thirteenth," "Lunar Eclipse," "Three Laps before Dark."

Lavanderia: A Mixed Load of Women, Wash and Word: "Iron Fetish."

Leaves of Poetry: A Book of Tree Poems: "Green."

Pennsylvania Prize Poems: "Vignettes on Love," "Shrine of Hormones," "Sunshine on the Snow," "The Art of Listening," "When I Was in San Francisco," "Chemo Day Three."

Pushing the Envelope: Epistolary Poems: "What Cancer Sounds Like."

River Poets Journal: "Return."

Red River Review: "Bruised," "Barriers," "Emptied," "Eavesdropping On the Wait Staff at IHOP," "At Sunset Memorial Funeral Home" "Opening Drawers," "Sleeping Hot," "Illusion."

Sandstorm Literary Journal: "Jack."

San Pedro River Review: "Monologue of a Paper Towel," "Out of the Darkness, "The Truth behind Once Upon a Time," and "Portrait of Contradiction."

The Stray Branch: "The Rinse Cycle."

Siblings: Our First Macrocosm: "In The Waiting Room."

The Southern Poetry Anthology, Volume VIII: Texas: "Room 339"

Sugared Water: "Lifting Mama."

Texas Poetry Calendar: "If Mozart Were a West Texan" "Dawson, Texas 1958."

Voices de la Luna: "Clipped," "Sweeping."

DEDICATION

*To my family and friends for their support and encouragement,
in loving memory of Tom White, who put the bat in my hand and
persuaded me to start swinging.*

GRATITUDE

Thank you Diane Frank for your continual gentle pushes and belief in my work.

Thank you Nancy Clark, Carol Hall, Marsha Dry, and Janette Sloper for your input and insight and the time you spent with my words.

Thank you Cindy Huyser for editing this collection of musings.

Thank you Melanie Gendron for the book cover design and illustrations.

Thank you Chris Walker for snapping the photo.

WAITING

As long as night inhales darkness
and morning exhales light,
as long as the ocean's wet teeth nibble
on the toes of sandy beaches,
as long as there is life, there will be poetry.

Life is a poem waiting to be written.

I. IN MAMA'S HOUSE

How time transfers things, the opening and closing of doors,
ways of counting— mother to child, child to mother.

THE HELP'S DAUGHTER

*What does it feel like to raise a white child when your own child's
at home being looked after by someone else?*
—Kathryn Stockett, *"The Help"*

Feelings were commodities sealed in dented cans,
sold in ten for a dollar baskets at "Safeway."
Too extravagant for a husbandless woman
with seven mouths to feed.
Had she taken the time to open them,
each of us would have died
from poverty's rusted toxins.
Sitters were luxuries afforded to those with incomes
above government cheese and powdered milk.
We guarded each other with the ferocity of a Doberman.

Before leaving to clean other people's houses
and wipe the little boss' feet,
she divvied up chores as though they were an inheritance
and instructed, *Don't leave the yard.*
But each child stepped off the sidewalk,
crossed the muddied lines of disobedience and adventure,
left to move about in the world.

At times, we half swept the floors, sloshed Pine Sol
scented water while mopping, left Comet streaks
on the back of the toilet bowl.
We folded the towels but stuffed underwear in the drawers,
fought over whose turn it was to do the dishes
or take clothes off the line and who ate the last cookie.
No one ever tattled and our prepared speeches for absolution
were cleaning rags we never used.

Now, without debate, we use her rags to wipe dust
she can no longer see, mop floors with the precision
of a Swiss watch maker, wash dishes and fold her laundry
as though this was our design in life—to tidy up her illness.

This evening when darkness comes out of retirement,
I hear my brothers talking to my sister on the cell phone,
moving through the house as though motion is a cure.
Mom sits on the towel-covered toilet seat and says,
Diane, you'll have to go faster than this. I'm cold,
as I smooth cream over her frail body.

I will my hands to move faster, but caution creeps
in my fingers, causes me to slow once again.
Before slipping the lilac cotton gown over her thin body,
I examine the testament of scars on her stomach
stretched into the lives of six children.
Her wrinkled, veined skin conceals seventy-eight years of living.
My eyes are glued to her back as though it is a magnet
pulling me through amazement.
There is no evidence of aging, diabetes, dialysis, decline,
and the desperate blows of survival.
Her skin is smooth and clear,
transparent as the moment she began
teaching us to live without her.

IN THIS HOUSE

Yesterday is a collection of lost stories
banished to live as lepers like these dust bunnies
congregating behind a maple-stained corner cabinet.
Their fuzzy gray heads conceal answers
to questions that will remain riddles.
I'm alone in this house, walls grieving,
groaning with sounds while I pick through Mama's life.
What pain to decide the importance
of things my mother worked so hard to get, to hide.

Like this family in the plastic windows
she once kept in her wallet.
The photos are dated before my birth.
I find this mystery family spiral-bound,
hidden in a drawer where she kept her insulin needles,
underwear and crumbling old chocolate candy kisses.
What's hidden beneath these smiles
she has tucked away?
Did the man pay her salary?
The woman make a list of her chores?
Did these boys leave a legacy
of toys for my brothers to inherit?
It's curious how time clutters facts and possessions,
causes them to mingle
in a space small enough for a pair of shoes,
but too large for the mind to comprehend.
I toss the drawer's contents
into a thirty-two gallon trash bag
and keep the mini photo album.
It's a souvenir from my mother's past,
a place I can never visit.

SWEEPING

This is second generation dirt.
A quiet interloper who stole
through Mama's windows,
smuggled in his family one grain at a time,
and camped on her curtains, baseboards,
and underneath the toupee of red carpet.

For hours, I sweep thirty years of rouge grains,
sift through kitchen and bathroom cabinets
and stashes of costume jewelry.
Fatigue slows my pace, opens my eyes.
I find a harem of butterflies as great as King Solomon's.
Each room is a haven
for these metal, plastic, and glass beauties.

I am in the kitchen where a dynasty of monarchs
alit on yellow canisters, dishtowels, and wall hangings.
I wrap them in newspaper with the dust
still covering them like soft skin.
My mother loves these nectar-feeding insects
as though she is one.
But age and illness have made her a chrysalis.
She pumps life through her wings with a new cane,
slowly shedding her wheelchair and walker.
When she lifts them to fly, I will have returned
this swept dirt back to the earth—praying
today is not the day diabetes will do the same to her.

EMPTIED

Each room yawns with emptiness
and ghosts of past desires creek
across stained gray linoleum floors.
Walls look as though locusts swarmed,
ate away grandchildren's faces,
poems and crosses. Nail holes, old paint
and silhouettes of picture frames are the remains
of my family's lineage.
Boxed, labeled, shipped, stored and rationed
for someone else's garage sale, pieces of us
scatter from Odessa's flat dusty stomach
to Austin's hilly head.

The refrigerator hums a melancholy melody
as I blink back tears, searching for memories.
A veil of mystery sits on the top shelf
of a bedroom closet—*Jewelry. Send to Austin.*
The words on the box are penned with my hand.
I don't remember putting it there, but do remember
the September afternoon she leaves
with a necklace of fear sagging around her frail neck.

The air is in rehab from a bulimic summer of drought.
Thin grass blemished with heat stalks us to Brady, Texas.
There, in a McDonald's parking lot, we meet
the topaz and amethyst stones in her mother's ring.
We greet, chat, and race the sun to evening
before the three of them drive away with Mama's
new life blowing from the exhaust pipes.

IN MY MOTHER'S OLD PURSE

They multiply like coat-hangers in a dark closet.
—Terri Anthony

Needs multiply like coat-hangers in a dark closet,
eat through our wool-cushioned day like pale moths.
Erasers cannot fit over their huge inked heads.
No cap or scarf, coat or glove,
comforter or blanket to keep them contained.
They spread themselves into years,
like this grocery list in my mother's old purse.

Fourteen years she's needed eggs and milk,
Tide and toilet paper, beets and cabbage,
cinnamon and cornbread.
Curious how her clothes stayed clean and her belly full,
even after the record of her need was tucked away
in the soft darkness of her purse.

DIAGNOSIS

Heaven must be like this, exactly like this: ramparts that only stop
when they want to—and still more sky beyond.
—Alan Birkelbach

What is beyond this diagnosis,
this sentence of living with *sugar*?
What is beyond the sky's wide brim?
Sugar, that's what my mother calls diabetes.
What a gentle name for a disease
that can rob a body of limb and sight,
tether it to a plastic vein.

Even when darkness covers its pale face,
the thread of its light is constantly unraveling
beginnings, as limitless as numbers.
There is no fragility in the fight,
sweetness in the struggle
to walk each morning with Sugar's heavy feet
trotting through the body like a thoroughbred,
dragging my mother towards statistics' giant walls.
Look at them, challenging my mother
to scale those rough numbers, daring her
to live beyond their predictions.

How beautiful! The way she flexes
the strength of her will, leaps,
makes her life greater than the sky's wide brim.

IN THE WAITING ROOM

The day is creased with anxiety.
The hospital's odorless walls
are framed with a dull quiet.
The sudden opening and closing
of a sliding glass door
is a monotone distraction.
We are a small flock of sheep
waiting in this brick pasture
for our mother to return from surgery.

Raymond, the first born, once rushed to fires
in his fireman's hat and big rubber boots.
When he was a teenager, he drove a fire red '65 Malibu.
Speed is not a luxury or an occupation now.
The Malibu is parked, the bunker gear retired.
A weakened back slows his pace.
He moves about with a sturdy folding metal walker
tricked-out with tennis balls on the rear legs.

James, the second born, paces—
rushing minutes that are stuck
in a slow pond of angst.
He is a soul-seeking missile,
finds a couple sitting against a far wall.
Concern rims his eyes
as he chats; he will know their story
before they leave.
As a boy, he was a gatherer—
collected history, friends, favor.

I am the third born, trying to find a poem
in the high white ceiling, worried expressions,
and humid air traipsing in and out of the glass doors.
Words are my crutch and solace, comforting

me as I flip through magazines.
A past conversation fills me
like this fertile field of fear we're grazing in.
I'm going to be a teacher's aide.
No, you're not. You're going to be a teacher.
Her words prevailed.

Chris, the fourth born, is still on the road.
Trepidation cannot push his foot above the speed limit.
The staves of caution and law guide him
like Mama's stern voice.
Duty is the bell around his neck,
responsibility the cord that binds.
I cannot see him, but I know his heart
is racing.

Vince, the last-born male, sits composed.
Since childhood, he has known calm.
He is insulted by time, refuses to rush
even when his cell phone is flashing.
His demeanor is serene, body stilled,
save his fingers—
they manipulate keys, reveal his worry.
Numbers drive him;
their predictability keep him anchored.

Kim, the youngest, rests her head
on her husband's shoulder.
Fatigue covers both of them like thick wool.
For six months they have nursed Mama back to health.
Their lives are connected like the plastic vein cycling
life through our mother's arm.

Mama was rolled in with two legs;
she will be rolled out with one.
We are waiting
to see who can hold back tears the longest.

LIFTING MAMA

A rude sun smears light over the bedroom window.
I wake with Mama singing; I love the morning.
Love. A word tossed around so much
it has dark circles around its eyes.
I love my socks, fingernails, the way ants follow a soul
from Carver Street to French Place.
Love is a little purple gnome
sitting on the dashboard of an old Chevrolet pick-up,
years of flaky rusted dandruff scratched on its hood.

I am fully awake now. I get to change my mind
and this resentment I have towards the sun.
Love is my sister's arms around mother's back.
With an ulcer eating her stomach, she says to Mom,
Put your arms around my neck, Mama. On the count of three.
One: They rock. Mom scoots forward.
Two: *Stop fighting me Mama. Let go of the rail.*
Mom kicks against fear with the leg that was left
on the surgeon's table.
Three: They are one, mother-daughter, cheeks connected
like an umbilical cord.
Mom's butt is lifted; I grab the pad and put it in the transfer chair.

How time transfers things, the opening and closing of doors,
ways of counting—mother to child, child to mother,
pumps to wheels, panties to diapers, pride to pain.
I will give you an orange dress, Mama.
It is the only color brave enough to carry your darkness
in its pocket.

It's dark now and how I wish the two of you were here with me,
flanking my sides as I walk down this gravel road
with a cocky moon climbing over my head.

CLIPPED

This is what someone with wings does when he knows he cannot fly...
—The Vista, by C. Dale Young

The legs are wings.
Yet little boys flap their arms,
pump them like slats,
and create their own jet sounds.
The propellers are in the feet
and wind is in the thighs that lift,
carry them through the clouds
of their imaginations.

Morphine is the fuel dripping in Mom's fuselage,
crippling her view from the cockpit.
It skews her memory and makes her hallucinate.
My sister is *I don't know*
and I am *The old lady in the shoe.*
Four plastic wristbands keep her grounded
in a small white room where machines debate
with high pitches.

Her name is reduced to fit between tiny bars
in a trio of the bands.
Nurses scan them with rectangles of light
to keep record of who she is and to engineer her healing.
She thrusts from side-to-side,
I just want to move,
but both wings are clipped now.
As she waits for the metal appendages,
she flies with her eyes, tears propelling her forward.

Sleep carries me by the neck.
It is a prowling lioness and I am her cub.
I feel myself lifted from a plastic blue recliner
and placed upright in front of a water-streaked mirror
opening and shutting my eyes
as though this motion will make clarity flesh.

I wash my face and try to brush away
last night's fusty air from my mouth.
Why do sadness and mirth,
dreams and nightmares,
breaking and mending
have the same stale taste in the morning?

The sides of his yellow untied hazard gown
make the hospital tech look like a canary
as he flaps around the room readying her for discharge.
He holds a bedpan in his blue-gloved hands
as he chirps into his cell phone,
This is Brandon. 339 is going home.

Fully dressed, but half clutched in the lioness' mouth,
I scan the room, start packing her things.
She is Mama, the pulse of my drive
and source of my stubbornness.
To call her mother is too stiff and formal.
At this moment, I wish for the silence
camped in her throat as I take a dress off the hanger
and ask her, *Mama where are your shoes?*
With a voice softer than her bed sheets
she answers, *I have no shoes.*

With regret roaring in my stomach,
I rub my face searching for a bruise
after the lioness drops me into consciousness.
I didn't know the weight of limbs until my heart fell
in the place where Mama's legs used to be.

COLD CORNBREAD

Mother tells her friends I am a good daughter.

My body is a *do not disturb* sign
as I watch the secondhand circle
around an apple-faced clock in my kitchen.
I monitor its movements as though its purpose
is far greater than dividing life into morning and evening.

The smoke detector wails a death warning!
Between blinking back last night's dream
and showering beneath the first hot stream of morning,
I burn breakfast—boiled eggs and toast.
Time betrayed me; I was convinced I had more of it.
I share this with only a few.
They laugh, not in disbelief,
but in confirmation; I am a poor cook.

Mama allows me to measure, but not cook
her Cream of Wheat. She's afraid I will make it lumpy.
I pour; she stirs, we both watch it boil in the pot's steel mouth.
The circular motion of the whisk creates a smooth
white landscape and laughter fills my stomach
like rolling hills.

These same few know my potted ivy is silk.
They are aware my brown thumb ended
the lives of geraniums, crocus, iris.
I make a vow never to end life this way again.
I am a poor gardener.

Even a smaller few know I make tasty cornbread.
My mother knows—loves it cold with milk.

She tells everyone I am a good daughter.

MEMOIR OF SHOES

This box packed with shoes
is the history of my mother's feet.
Will these soles continue to tell her story
after this container is hauled away?
Especially this pair of black pumps
she wore to church.
The throat of one has a tiny scar.
Dye can conceal the bruised place,
but what of her memoir?
Can they voice how her heels rubbed
against the quarters, pressed down
the hard edges of single motherhood?
How can they, without a tongue?

Will the new owners feel the pen of her feet?
Decipher a scribbled Sunday morning
filled with passion and perspiration?
Survive the heated hands of a West Texas July
pressed against church pews and walls?
Hear the water of her soprano voice
splash *Amazing Grace* over the sanctuary?

Listen to the congregation wave their fans,
pray for the gospel of a cool breeze,
as the choruses of God's mercy leak out
the raised windows?

WORDS FLOATING FACE UP

He wanted to call the stars back,
tell them not to dot the sky just yet.
—*Mary Karr*

The night is impressed with itself,
showing off a smile with a mouth full
of brilliant teeth!
Enchanted by its ebony beauty,
I swear off wearing black again.
But I cannot unbutton my skin
or hang it in the closet between
sleeveless blouses and stone-washed jeans.
I am dressed in blackness and will be
as long as the night is the night.
I'm not ready for the stars to recede
back into the ocean of day.

Let them bite through the darkness.
Maybe they can help me find answers
on that tongue of clouds
whispering towards the moon.

I want to know what/who can impress these stars.
Mama's name is not heavy enough
Seventy-nine, she is powerful enough
to learn to walk without legs made of bones and flesh
and make her words float face up
in the aged boat of her strength.

THE ART OF LISTENING

My desire—the sacrament of song,
the hymns of my youth, the holiness of listening,
hear the covenant concession between heart and ears.

I miss the sound of my mother singing.
I miss the music of who she is.
I am trying to get it on paper,
but I am failing at it.

When I was a child, my smile went on a rampage
as I listened to her voice rise and fall
over the cliff of morning.

Now Mother is asleep; her chest rises and falls
as a trumpet of wind blows carols
through a scorched evergreen.

A chorale of stars gathers overhead,
melody pitched so high
notes look like pins of light
scattered across the staff of sky.

And I am on the patio in a plastic green chair,
reclining in the lap of an armless night.
Holding myself, I let my eyes dance across the moon
while I listen to the melody of a car's engine
ricochet in the corridors of darkness.

MAMA'S HANDS

Clouds are decimals.
—Davis Joseph Remington Clarke

The river is an acolyte at the altar of morning.
Clouds are decimals
and Mama's hands are hybrids.

The movement of her long fingers is a melody,
a tempo marking of largo.
With dusk-veiled eyes she loops and pulls
strands of soft plaid fabric, knotting the edges
of the no-sew blankets we craft together
to donate to the Texas Oncology Center.

Protruding veins in the music of her hands
pull me back to the time when my language was a river
of babble and I was too young to count the clouds.

She carried me like a blanket on her shoulders.
Her palms bound me to her chest as my fingers
went on reconnaissance in the nape of her neck.

After eighty years, her hands still bind me to her chest
as I watch her prop elbows on the padded armrests of her wheelchair.
She rests with palms hovering over the soft plaid fabric
like a Monet sunrise.

VISITATION

It's early Sunday afternoon in this desert city of Odessa.
Winter is sovereign, but today, the sun
kicks against the cold with its warm yellow boots.
Mom hugs her sweater close to her body
before moving from the wheelchair to the walker.
I stand behind her, a smile plastered on my face
as a pail of dim light spills over the threshold.
My voice is a bell ringing bliss as I babble about boxes,
pictures, patio furniture, appliances. . .
Six years she has not visited the sanctuary of my home,
communed with me in the space of my living.
But this afternoon we look at the backyard
with its large deck and bald lawn—I speak of its future beauty.
She listens to the melody of wind-chimes, suggests I get more.
We both skip those six years like smooth stones over the river of time.

II. PORTRAITS

The night is my sister.
We both wear the skin of darkness,
hum music of the wind.

SISTERS

You are a child of the universe, no less than the trees and the stars...
—Max Ehrmann

The night is my sister.
We both wear the skin of darkness,
hum music of the wind,
clutch leaves of love in our hands like currency,
carry the heat of stars in our mouths.

We fold the desire of respect
in our long arms like fresh laundry,
and watch the moon, that round tiara of light,
crown our heads with such conviction
it dares anyone to challenge
the beauty of our blackness.

THREE LAPS BEFORE DARK

Last week, a surplus of sun.
Today, a cache of cold and drizzle,
a mélange of melodies from grackles
camped in a bulky pine.

We compete with a frosty wobbly wind
as we tread our way through the flapping flags
lined along the path in Memorial Garden Park.
A hungry clique of ducks waddle onto the grass,
but we have no bread crumbs to give.
With empty hands stuffed in our pockets, we side-step.
Me, the big sister. You, the little sister,
as we walk in scraggly light.

Look. I point out patina colored statues—
a little girl somersaulting, a boy crawling through a log
and two children playing leap frog, their dog a spectator.

We chatter continuously, catching up on the last few months
as darkness chases us around the park.
On the last lap, you hug your jacket tighter; I unzip mine
as my body tangles with Tamoxifen-induced heat.
Three fortunate pigeons swoop down, peck on donated dinner
as we admire the bronze girl seated with her legs crossed.
A laurel of banana-colored mums makes ruffles
around the hem of her skirt.

Her beauty is a feeble bastion,
too frail to hold our attention.
We walk on, watch the darkness
chew through an amuse-bouche of light,
and night poke the final holes in this soft day.

RENEGOTIATION

It's hard to breathe within the space created by never.
—Rick Rigsby

It's hard to breathe within the space created by never,
fill the lungs with emptiness,
live with a heart pumping dismal predictions.
But look at Rick, running through life
with success on his heels,
kicking gravel at committee members
of the "they said you can't" statistical society.

He altered circumstance's dark suit,
ripped its condemning shoulder seams,
replaced grim buttons with a gold zipper
shining like a medal,
and monogrammed his cuffs with
Don't tell me it's impossible.

Here I am in lipstick redder than a harlot's,
flirting with the same board he fled,
skirt lifted as though confidence is a garter.

I want to renegotiate destiny's terms,
pick plums from my neighbor's tree,
play outside past dark and break
criticism's rotten teeth.

I want to learn to tie a double-knot
in the type of thick hairy rope
neighborhood kids used to hang old car tires on.

I want to tuck my body in the belly of one of those old tires
then swing until I am back in my mother's womb,

right before the moment of my birth.
This time when the midwife says push,
I would come out swinging, pitch my legs
above clothesline poles, fear, condemnation,
and kick my heels past the world's invisible fence.

GREEN

When I was younger, I knew trees—
not their names,
but the veins of green leaves,
configurations of branches,
vulnerability of tender twigs.
I climbed them, even though girls
were not encouraged to do such boyish things.

In summer, when green was plump,
filled with the heft of budding life on maples,
oaks, pecans, I watched boys
share secrets in cocoons of leaves.
I wanted to share my secrets, too,
but was not allowed into their sanctuary.

On this October morning,
having breakfast at a restaurant,
I stare at an unknown tree outside,
its half-naked limbs posed like bare muscles.
The green, like a chameleon,
now turning orange, crimson
a sleepy amber, fused in receding leaves.

In winter, those leaves will wither,
and be no more.
This poem is a record of their existence,
before they disappear like the Garden of Eden.

THE COLD ARMS OF JUNE

Education is the ability to listen to almost anything
without losing your temper or your self-confidence
                    —Robert Frost

In West Texas, June spits out temperatures
of one hundred degrees or more.
Night is soaked with spicy air.
Rain is elusive and yellow, a metaphor for grass.

On the Big Mountain, June's arms are cold.
A wall of snow fifteen feet high surrounds Paradise Inn.
As darkness descends, precipitation drools on leaves,
the street, my vacation.

Immersed in silence, I sip hot apple cider,
listen to floors creak in the lodge,
long for warmer clothes.

I stare beyond the sun setting on icy slopes,
pine trees, the night's white armor,
stare until I see a girl sitting at my fourth grade desk,
listening to whispered insults, teasing as paralyzing
as the cold, her tears frozen—invisible.

I return to my tearless silence,
wonder if Rainier's puffy white eye watched
St. Helens' spit flameless orange fire from her guts.
She spewed fury, leaving miles of earth barren
before the winds swallowed her rage.

I feel her wet rage
before maturity spills through my eyes.
Had the little girl known St. Helens' power
and Rainier's beauty, she wouldn't have cried
when other kids teased,
You're as tall as a mountain.

FLINTSTONES AT THE OLIVE GARDEN

All sitcoms are based on the Flintstones.
Fred spends his time scheming and Wilma forgives him.
—Paul DuPont

I laughed at Fred's schemes when I was a child
and at a lady in our congregation.
Licks of gray sticky in her wiry black hair,
her eyes asking questions only the universe could answer,
"Simple," Mama called her.

I regret that now.
She played chords that had not been created
on an old guitar she bought at a garage sale.
When she started singing, my laughing tears
could not hear her heart.

But I heard children laugh when I fell hard
on the playground's red dirt.
Tammy tripped me, made me the star of her anger,
used my humiliation to slay her demons.
Her smooth ebony skin shining with relief
made me choose:
Remain on the ground stained with shame or stand.

I stand forgiving.

FROM THE DIARY OF QUEEN VASHTI:
A LETTER TO ESTHER

Dear Esther:

I do not speak with the tongue of Narcissus.
My loveliness is like the wine-stained goblets
that littered the guest tables of my husband—our husband.
Vanity did not bind me to my chambers that night—
The Creator did.
He would not allow the folly of a man to soil my crown
or auction my dignity to an ogling drunk.

After the sun lifted the lid of darkness,
and the red of too much wine drained from his eyes,
Xerxes would have remembered all of those men
touching me with their stares, violating me with lust.
The strength of my resolve spared me from this shame.

Should this be the fate of a queen?
To never again feel the breath of her king
rise and fall as morning against her cheek
Morning is a false soothsayer; it blinds you to the club of pain.
When that first blow strikes your knees, shock steals your voice.

The scent of trampled olives lingers outside my window.
I miss the potters' birds, mountain goats etched in walls,
the fragrance of the palace gardens.
I have no maiden to stave off this heat
swarming around my arms.
I hear you have seven.
What favor you have found with our beloved?

Caution, my young counterpart with your lovely figure
and white dove beauty; beware of banquets.
Destruction squeezes its plump head into the belly of grapes,
it waits to be pressed into the wine of celebration.
Before you take that first drink, know
I'm exiled so you can carry the weight of my crown.

A LETTER TO THE WOMAN IN THE BLACK DRESS
STANDING NEAR THE WINDOW

I don't know how to transpose the music of quails,
interpret the language of goats,
or use words to draw the expression on your face.

It's not loneliness. Loneliness is round like a hole
waiting to be filled with mud-thick darkness
or emptiness so deep it echoes.

It's not peace. Peace is a rectangle
stretched on a canvas with the silhouette of winter
napping on the front porch.

The snow is orderly, perfectly shaped to induce tranquility.
Your face is a square delicate field
irrigated with rows of questions.
What is stilling your body,
fixing your eyes like an owl's?

Outside my window the wind is tiptoeing,
rummaging through battered pines—
searching the archives of its branches for artifacts,
dropping pinecones and sparrow feathers.
Its long hair is tangled in the string of wind chimes.

Lady, your black dress is a distraction,
the hem barely legal over the trunk of your thighs.
Your dress, like you, roars for attention.
Did you read the sign above your head?
Quiet please. Let others enjoy the silence.

DRIED MILK

Morning still has its youthful face.
I am in the library chatting with a friend
before we both start our day.
He comes in gliding as though his feet are made of joy.
The corners of his happy mouth wear remnants
of breakfast, milk and sausage biscuits.
Head moving up and down like a rocking horse,
he draws books from a bucket
and places them on a cart.
Everything in him blinks happiness.
Guess what?

I am wondering
what can make his six-year-old eyes beam
with such delight?
My friend is wondering, too.
We got our electricity turned back on!
"That's great," she says.

My throat is thick with memory.
I know such poverty, grew up that way.
I ran from it, hate for hardship wild in my eyes.
It slept with me, fed me everything
in its empty pockets.

Poverty filled my eyes with longing
for windows with clean curtains,
running water, a balance in the checkbook
that would keep my Mama out of the pawn shop.

Precious child, poverty caught my mother and yours.
When it chases you, run hard,
with hate for it wild in your eyes.

SEEKING SMOOTH AIR

Fear is a long thin tongue licking at the sky
as the wind empties its pockets,
shakes them until cold air tumbles out.
I clutch a stranger's arm the way I would a lover's
when the constant shaking feels like a bucking horse.

Stewardesses harness themselves,
backs flat as books.
The brunette attendant glances in my direction
with a practiced smile.
Ladies and gentlemen please remain in your seats
and keep those seat belts fastened.
We are seeking smooth air.
The flash of her teeth does not calm me.
My feet move like they are on a trampoline
and my fists roll into themselves like meatballs
as the pilot pushes the blue nose forward.

Where is such air?
Does the pilot see soft straight lines
thirty thousand feet above ground?
Or are they broken
like the fading white lanes on my street?

When I was a child, I gazed upwards,
wishing my arms were wings
and my feet could kick against the wind
to lift me out of a darkness I did not understand.
I wanted to be among those drifting white chameleons
over my head. Now I am among them,
but their puffy heads are flat and gray.
And so it is with longing, wishing for something
other than what you have.

I want to be on the ground—
a place where I have tricked myself into believing
I am in control.

REVELATION IN FLIGHT

The flight from Odessa to Dallas has enough emptiness
for each passenger to have their own domain of elbow space.
I snuggle in the window seat, the cool glass a lullaby
on my warm cheek.
Miss Busy Bee, soon to be Mrs., stirs the silence
in my hive when she drops her belongings
and chatter next to me.
My eyes are pliers pulling the wings
from her twenty-something back.
I can feel the stickiness
as I listen to *Honey will you please check on…*
We need… There should be… Thank you so much baby…
I love you.

When the flight attendant makes *the* announcement
that requires interaction between passengers only,
she looks at me.
Joy floats on light
in a pair of brown irises searching a stranger's face
for confirmation.
I give her a smile then fall asleep
with the edges of the sun creasing my mouth and her natter
about three hundred envelopes buzzing in my ear.

SHRINE OF HORMONES

Love is old as the earth.
You think I am old as the earth
and know nothing of love.

You still believe we— your parents—
held hands then you were born.
To imagine our bodies bare,
touching, melting in love's red flame
is to say air is the color of pineapple.

I know its euphoria, betrayal
the epic of coming together, going apart
and I know your booming voice, riotous laugh
are camouflaged anger.

Your belly ripples when you tell stories
of your jock friends, how they get the girls,
and will not leave you leftovers.
Those are angry words
you bite with the grace of a swan.

Love ignites the flame of jealousy's bonfire.
It comes back to her; she walks away with your heart,
chasing the most popular, the most handsome— this girl
you worship in the shrine of your hormones.

Son, you are fourteen, love is not a red flame;
it is a thin reed— your first heartbreak.
My ears sting with your vow, "She's the last one!"

Because I love you more than the day you were born,
I will not tell you she is just the beginning.

RETIREMENT COLORS

The weekend is two days past its prime
when an electronic whistle resurrects her
from a sleep that resembles death's limp arms.
Morning is robust with light.
She squints at her first encounter with the day,
the sun squeezing its stout head
through slits in the vertical blinds.
Her gluteus, biceps and thighs ache like a bad tooth.
Yesterday she spent an hour jerking, jumping,
bumping, pumping, grinding her hips doing Zumba.
She moved her body with Latin rhythms
as though they were a hypnotist.

Here she is, a retired debutant
gyrating like a twenty-something.
Her white homemade gown
is stained with thirty years of memories
packed away in a place she cannot remember.

Her fingers dance
across a photo album,
across plastic sheathed memories,
across the picture where she is waltzing
with her eldest brother—
both of their hair dyed black with youth,
backs erect with social expectations.

The gray that has slithered stealthily in her crown
does not bring longing for that teenage queen.
She knows she cannot retrieve this girl
and doesn't want to.

She closes her eyes and returns to the cave of sleep
with her shoes at the foot of the bed.
They are like two opened mouths waiting to be filled.

DO NOT DISTURB A POEM

It's not polite to interrupt a poem.
Let her go through the ritual of becoming
before you put her to the blade—
the washing of her face in mysteries,
the plucking of adjectives from her arched brows,
the soaking in a lavender bath of images
until her layers of skin wrinkle with words,
adorning those long braided sentences
snaking from her lovely head with colorful beads.

When she puts on her reading glasses
and cotton jacket lined with similes,
do not offer a goodbye. Ask where she's going
or how long it will take. Peel potatoes and dice an onion.
She may take a long stroll across the shelves
to visit Mary, Elizabeth, or Emily.
Leave her warm seat alone;
you can gather the crumbs of her thoughts later.
Do not touch that basket of verbs next to her pen.
Poem's been eating from it all morning.

Finish cooking the soup if she falls prey to a nap
and dream of dipping her foot in Cinderella's abandoned shoe.
It will not fit; that slipper is too narrow for her thinking.
Poem would not run from love, power, time or magic.
She would stand in the middle of the palace
and allow midnight to chime in her
soiled clothes, rough hands, and combat boots.
She would ask the prince to dance.
If he refused, she would walk away
leaving him with a withered pumpkin, hungry mice
and her name waltzing about his arrogant heels.

ILLUSION

What is so utterly invisible as tomorrow?
—Mary Oliver

I treat tomorrow with long locks of certainty
and strong arms that will embrace "the five year plan."
I give it elaborate names like calendar,
agenda, itinerary, next year,
expect it to squeeze my shoulders,
massage plans into perfection and fill its basket
with unfinished business.

I try to tie a weight around its veiled neck
to anchor my need for security
up and down the stairs of my mind.

I treat it as though I own it,
can make it do tricks at the snap of fingers.
How I deceive myself!
I am on the porch of evening,
an expectant puppy wagging her hope,
paws scratching towards a sky freckled with light,
waiting for tomorrow to rub me on my head.

HAND WOVEN

Her body is a basket
crafted of tendons and bones
muscles and blood.

Her mother's words are tiny reeds
woven into her spine.
She feels them in the handle of her long memory.
With an erect back, she chews her bottom lip,
uses a pencil like a needle
as she stitches sentences together.

Darkness is a heavy lid over the sky
as the Dollar Store clock blinks four a.m.
Her fingers quarrel with a mob of curly hair
as she brushes her hand across her head,
and think about the quarrel she had with her mother.
A lady does not tattoo her body.

She carries a constellation of black stars
on her smooth bamboo colored arms.
Its tail dips below the straight edge of her cuffed sleeve
as she shuts off lights
and tucks herself into the static of sleep.

I AM A WOMAN

I am a pair of gold cufflinks
clamped in the long sleeves of a white tuxedoed day.
Even as the sky cradles the sun,
I fasten the sunrise
in the soft seams of milky natal mornings.
And night, the lesser of gentlemen,
loosens my toggles and forces my head
through the perfectly slashed cuff slits.
We do this ritual of dressing/undressing
like we have since the River Euphrates
opened her skirt.

I am a rib,
the feathered-hat man is missing.
He sees me as flesh,
but he knows under the bones of my power,
I am a woman.

WHEN THE HEART HAS WINGS

"I lost my family."
He says it as though he misplaced them
in the garage or they fell through the crack
in between the washer and dryer.
"Drugs. Needed somethin' to help me sleep.
Lost a couple of good jobs, too.
Been workin' steady now."
His eyes rake across the falling light
of day as he holds her hand.

A wave of compassion crosses her face;
she knows the Vietnam war
has created an assembly line of insomniacs.
He bites into her pity like a ripe pear.
"I'm a good man."

Her father asks, "How do you attract
those with such hard luck?
When it comes to the heart, she is a jet.
Air does not have flashing scarlet lights,
or amber diamond-shape SLOW signs.
Love, that naive pilot, speeds into headwinds,
disregarding the control tower of reason.

Twenty years, their souls ride
through the turbulence of marriage,
still holding hands, flying with joy.

A PORTRAIT OF CONTRADICTIONS

This moment is a corral of wild horses
bucking against the fence.
One of my blue-eyed stallions threatening
to slip the reins of control from my hands.
I try to bridle his laughter, pull him back.
I put a sharp edge in my voice
in hopes to spook him into submission.
What is wrong with you? What's so funny?
He cracks with a small West Texas drawl,
I am just so sad I am laughing in my pants.
I look past my agenda, lesson plans
to see a rough rim of misery
on his smooth eight-year old face.
Divorce is riding on the horizon.
He's in the saddle waiting to dismount—
second rodeo for both parents.
Too young to wash his sorrows in a bottle
of Jim Beam, he laughs himself into tears,
rehearsing to slip into that skin of toughness
his Daddy demands he wears.

IF MOZART WERE A WEST TEXAN

He'd adorn his upper lip with a mustache.
Crown his head with a rust Roxbury Stetson.
Swath his feet with snake skin boots.
Design his butt with a pair of tight Levi's.
Wear a white button-down starched
crispier than a corn-shell taco.

He'd eat cheese enchiladas and drink sweet tea
after a frozen strawberry margarita appetizer.
Tip the waitress generously with paper currency
and leave twelve quarters in his water glass
for the busboy.

He'd drive home in his silver Ford F-250 pickup truck.
Sit in his La-Z-Boy near the living-room window
where the desert's rough face presses against the glass.
Watch the sky's kennel of color change
from Golden Retriever to Irish Red Setter.

At sunset, he'd listen to Bach's Suite No. 3 en ré majeur
(in D Major)
while night, a black wolf, howled on the horizon
and licked up light.
He'd study a dark constellation of grackles
strung out on telephone wires.

Then he'd tilt his head covetously towards his fallen star,
Maria Constanze, the desire in his throat grittier
than the red West Texas sand clinging to his boots.
He'd close his eyes as she leaned over a sink of dishes,
humming while soap bubbles rose around her difficult hands
like a lazy moon.

BARBARA

For Barbara Hall on her 70th birthday.

Age is an apprentice of beauty.
She does not argue with the seventy years
stealing into the knuckles of her hands
as she turns the glossy leaf of a magazine.
She points to a page; we both lean in
and ogle at plush décor neither of us desire.

I look at the hive of white hair spun neatly on her head
and wonder how many pages she has turned?
How many words she's collected since her birth?
How many times has she skimmed over the posh
in favor of a smile from a child, laughter from a friend,
the quiet gathering of family?

She is unpretentious as the moonflower.
It sleeps with its loveliness furled inwards,
away from the spotlight of the sun.
But when the quiet light of evening
slips on a pair of soft dark loafers,
that flower opens with its trumpet vines
blasting beauty into the long chorus of night.

CAROL

For Carol Hall on her 70th birthday

Years are the back roads of memories.
She packs seventy of them in the trunk of her body,
brings them to the meadow of our friendship.

I unpack boxes, a newspaper clipping of her slips
from a plastic window in my scrapbook.
A helmet of curls frames her seven-year old face.
She poses, a leader, in her rhythm band uniform.
Cadences of mystery tap across her closed-mouth smile.
Her eyes are sojourners wandering over the long plains of time.
I hold the picture in my hand, wonder what she was like as a child.
Did she let rain's fragrance soak her locks?
Play in fertile East Texas mud?
Listen to chattering between wind and leaves?

April's air is a spring convert. She'll plant a garden,
feed hummingbirds, fill her soul with words.
When day closes its one big orange eye,
she'll trade the tenderness of her green thumbs
for the rough ways of *Alaska: The Last Frontier.*

How did this leader of the band grow
to love the frowzy demeanor of the wilderness?
March into the life of an anxious first year teacher?
Beat her drum with compassion through a revolution of change?
The answers hang like fuzzy dice on the past's rearview mirror.

Her uniform is memory, mane is straight, smile is wide
and her eyes still wander over the long plains of time
searching for more years to ride.

III. IN OTHER PEOPLE'S KITCHENS

Hunger is a snare drum rattling in my stomach!
And pain is a cleaver chopping away those things
that keep us bound to our past.

EAVESDROPPING ON THE WAITSTAFF AT IHOP

The tang of coffee, pecan syrup, smoke
and bleach hovers over blue vinyl seats.
I am a part of the blue, the leftover odors
tiptoeing up my sleeves
and invisible to the six waitresses
occupying two booths behind me.

They are like a collection of Thursdays,
a day we bulldoze to get to Friday.
There are no ballads or poems
romanticizing its arrival.
The prefix is too needy,
too close to thirsty.
I am thirsty listening to them, but afraid
to disturb their intimacy.

I want a little girl.
How come you won't have one?
I already have two kids and trying
to get child support from two daddies.
I want to wait until I get married
before I have the third one.
Well, make sure he is rich.
Paying income taxes is hell.

It's four o'clock and I need to be. . .
need to be. . .somewhere although I forget.
Hunger is a snare drum rattling in my stomach!
My tongue taps out, "Excuse me."
I hope the cadence of my words
will not put a wrinkle in her fate,
or keep her from meeting Mr. Friday.

BARRIERS

That makes me as happy as hash browns and brownies.
—Jeremy Witherspoon

His four-year-old smile is the flesh of innocence
while he dangles his legs like a ragdoll.
The view from his mother's hip is better,
the world safer, kinder, smaller near her heart.
To see the sky with arms wrapped around her neck
is happiness like hash browns and brownies.

Not like the taste of fear in my mouth
as I watch this politician running with spite on his heels.
His words are harpoons aimed at the vulnerable.
How he desires to wash away the poor,
sweep them under the stoop of arrogance,
spray them with a hose of insignificance,
drain into the sewage of nonexistence.
He would let all of us in the middle—
the ones with two slices of bread and no butter,
collect toothpicks to build new cities.

For those with enough but cannot buy a country,
what fate will he assign them?
If we all disappear, return to that place before conception
where earth and water are not separate,
what will be wealth's measuring rod?

A green lady stands at the shore,
her flamed hand burning with hope,
broken shackles of oppression and cruelty at her feet.
Oh, how this soul desires to sit on her hip
and listen to the stories of dreams rolling
in and out to sea.

FULL OF EMPTY ROOM

The hands on my watch are cymbals
crashing for seven minutes.
I feel her before I see her—
the waitress at La Esperanza Restaurant.

She makes no apologies,
stares at my hands like my fingers are broken glass,
afraid I will cut myself, hemorrhage loneliness.

I do not tell her my frustrations—
impatience with thievery,
the scandal that makes my tongue a straight razor.

Instead, I focus on the busboy
pushing a metal cart toward the kitchen,
knives and forks clattering,
plates clanging glassy rhythms,
and I eavesdrop on a family two tables over.

I am still hungry; my stomach is full of empty room
a little girl tells her mother—
taco in one hand, forkful of beans in the other.
I watch her eat, feel my anger drain into dark tea.
If my courage were a rock, I would tell her
not to fill her dreams with frivolous things.

THE DRIVE-THROUGH WINDOW
AT CHURCH'S CHICKEN

The drive-through window
at Church's Chicken is crammed
with cars wrapped around the building
like Christmas tree lights.

Heavy frost on my windshield
does not complain about the line,
lingering cold or an empty stomach.
I do.

Smoke pirouetting around a half-lit cigarette butt
entertains me before it dances its way into a river
of smoke flowing from the exhaust of a gray Chevy
ahead of me.

My turn! I order two fish platters
with coleslaw, mashed potatoes instead of fries.
I come home with dinner
when you make your announcement.

You ask, *Why are you angry?*
Be calm, you say.

I gave you my heart.
You grew in confidence,
climbed the corporate ladder,
accumulated more on my backbone,
with my push, my sacrifices.

And you are going to eat from *her* table
after I sat at the cold drive-through window
at Church's Chicken?

BURNT TOAST AND HEAVY STARCH

Maybe the toast is a little burnt,
egg yolks runnier than you prefer.
I am a lousy cook, but a good wife.

The kids are bathed.
I washed your clothes,
ironed your shirts with heavy starch
just the way you like them— I thought.
I would have used less
had I known of your dissatisfaction.

I bump into you and the one
who makes a perfect breakfast.
You scratch your neck.
Don't blame your itch
on my cooking and Faultless Starch.

The brown on her toast is perfect;
she can sure fry eggs!
You love the smell of breakfast
coming from her kitchen.
After fourteen years and two kids,
will her eggs be too runny?

THREE STAGES OF SILENCE

1.
I weigh my words on caution's scale,
select them the way I would a ripe plum,
balance each one on my tongue's soft tip.
I roll them on the roof of my mouth
before I give them to you—
your silence covers me
like hard crashing waves.

2.
I try sleeping, but torrential silence
pounds on my pillows and echoes in my ears.
I strain to hear something, anything
until my muscles are sore.
The struggle ends in sleep.

3.
I wake, your icy expression
frozen in my mind.
I pour hot tea over ice,
watch it melt your face
clear, hard.
I stir sugar in a dark abyss,
drink in yesterday,
drown my throat with silence.

LUNAR ECLIPSE

A yard of hard red sand clutching clumps of weeds
and a few blades of stubborn yellow grass.
The house's pink skin flakes with age.
A few shingles look like chipped teeth.

A smack of light bruises the Mrs.' cheeks
as her eyes surf the dingy darkness
through an opened kitchen window
where the moon rests
after hiking the wide trail of sky.
That's easier than watching the gray Sedan
roll backwards from the graveled drive.
She and the Mr. started lumbering backwards
after the lay-off, after the bottle, after *her*.

His lone headlights are long gashes in the night.
The fatigue of rolling for miles
makes him think when
if he returns maybe he will replace the shingles, water the yard
and repair what was broken between them.

AFTER THE FIRST SNOW

"with such cheer as even the leaf must wear
as it unfurls its fragrant body. . ." —Mary Oliver

Stars climb out of the soft night,
tenderly burn as the last hem of day vanishes.

Cold air tumbles down the hill of sky
and settles spread-eagle over my doorframe.

The light from my neighbor's television shines
through the window like a blue beacon.

You tell me what I ask of you is too hard.
I lock the conversation in the cellar of my tongue.

The harsh cuffs of despair are your jailor.
You tell me what you can't do.

The tree does not say to the leaf,
do not unfurl your fragrant body.

The wind does not say to the grackle,
alter the shrill in your frosty song.

The soul does not say to man,
do not breathe you are a stone.

I say to you, do not debate with me.
Make the charcoal shine.

Sometimes the only thing we have left
is the rubbing of our fingers
against the impossible.

THE RINSE CYCLE

Laundry day. Sheets of sunshine cover fall's chilly breath.
Wind hovers, stalks disconnected leaves.
She sweeps away dried discolored refugees from beneath her eaves.

Sorting ritual in place,
    she sifts through clothes, linens, yesterday,
    unattached socks, begs the whisky bottle for a pardon,
    separates darks from lights,
imagines the day or night you were never born.

Late afternoon. Bed still not stripped.
She grinds her teeth, fumbles through half
the day with an excuse cocktail and drawn curtains.

They remain that way while she peels layers of regret
from the mattress, dusts the mobile your baby teeth never touched.

The odor of guilt staggers across the ceiling like arthritic pain.
Did you know it smells like spoiled milk,
feels like two hundred dollars?
Spinning ceased. Rinse cycle finished.
Laundry room hallowed with silence
like the hollowness of an empty womb,

She uses the bathroom curtain rod to hang laundry,
dries the tears she cries for the day or night you were never born,
crawls past her discomfort, listens—
hears stones echo a lullaby through leaves
disconnected from barren trees like her.

She touches her belly, wonders where you are,
if you are covered for warmth,
     safe from the plunge you will never take,
     prays one day you will understand the reason
for the day or night you were never born.

Truth affixes itself to dryer sheets; she folds it with the towels.

JACK

For Tom White—here's to keeping promises

Jack Daniel's been feasting on liver,
without onions, since before the depression.
Luminous amber in a glass carriage
he makes an entrance with an entourage
of dark rich colas into a tenth wedding anniversary.
Celebration day, six white roses sprawled
across the kitchen table, a box of half-eaten chocolates,
a smokeless candle, Jack and a sandy-haired child watch
volcanoes of clouds spew cold gushes of rain.
"Mommy, can I play outside?"

Mommy hears only the buzz of Jack.
He answers for her, "Sure."
Without Jack, Mommy would never let her play alone
beneath volcanic drops of rain or the places
where sidewalks and streets meet.
Anniversary celebration ends with drool
on couch cushions and silence creeping
up and down stairs.
Screaming sirens interrupt silence, celebration, life.

"Where's the baby?"

A tall thin man dressed in a sullen expression,
and a short round woman with two dark moles
underneath her left eye sit in a white rectangular
room filled with smells of sanitized purity
and a hint of Jack's stale cologne.
Payment policies and insurance solicitations hang
on the west wall above a row of blue cushioned chairs.

One worn brown shoe turned on its side exposes an uneven
heel, disconnected sole; its counterpart dangles
from the foot of the short woman.
Anxiously she rocks with head in hands,
bangs draped over her short fingertips.
He sits straight, draws in long shallow breaths,
peers at the west wall.

SUNSHINE ON THE SNOW

For Bob and Barbara Scribner

Even after all this time
The sun never says to the earth "you owe me."
Look what happens with a Love like that!
—It lights the whole Sky. (Hafiz)

Years tumble from branches of time
like falling leaves,
changing, collecting, gathering
until they are piled into gold mysteries.
But you say there is no secret.

Morning conversations are preludes
to love's long day of gestures, hugs
and the way they coil into silent rhythms.

You tell me this is how you stay married
for fifty years.
Honor the space between shared memories,
remember the first air of spring;
it is like a first touch
and that it comes after winter's
cold stones of trials.

Always, always keep your hands open
so you can learn to let go and welcome
the warmth life has to offer
even as sunshine on snow.

VIGNETTES ON LOVE

1

My soul went in search of you
not with promises or trinkets
but with a white flag of surrender.
In the morning dew, I surrendered myself
to fields of bluebonnets, Indian paintbrushes,
pink evening primroses—you, love.

2

Curled on the sofa,
our souls mingle, bond
between breaths.
We inhale, exhale— love.

3

Early morning light creeps
through an open window,
gently tickles, opens our sleeping eyes
with its placid fingers.
We exchange soft greetings, drowsy smiles
our fingers knotted in love's strength.

THE WAY HE SEES HER

He sees her as a reflection,
an echo rumbling across
the slick glass of a mirror.
He doesn't understand why she moves
a perfect steak on her plate like a chess pawn,
tips her fork away from it,
refuses to feast on his choice,
would rather eat air than taste his arrogance.

He assumes because a stranger cannot
tell the difference from their moon-lid eyes,
the gentle curve of their noses,
and perfectly symmetrical lips.
He doesn't understand the mystery
of their bond, the pact they made in the womb
when the two of them swam limb-to-limb
in that small wet world.

They played, kicked, each other
in a place where the memory of their beginning
followed them in the umbilical cord.
She was the first to feel the sting of dry life,
kicked feet in a hive of light,
knew the wings of loneliness.
Her first cry was a decree to keep the other safe.

Thirty years later she keeps her vow
with a pat of butter.
For thirty minutes he buzzed with complaint,
"How can you forget I like my rolls dry?"
Had he looked her in the eyes, he would have seen
the two minute difference in the pair staring at him,
carving an exit sign on his forehead.

IRON FETISH

I have a fetish for irons.
I like to listen to them hiss,
sputter white clouds of moisture
while they press wrinkles
out and creases into my clothes.
The heavier, steamier
they are—the sexier.
How can science be so beautiful—
the combination of heat and pressure?
Heat and pressure. Heat and pressure.
Stunning. Simply stunning.

When I turn on an aluminum and steel goddess,
move it over a white cotton or blue linen blouse
or a pair of jeans wet with heavy Niagara spray starch,
my pulse races with excitement.
My fingers grip the handle as though we are old lovers.
I've had a harem over the years,
Singer, General Electric, Emerson
and loved each one.
But. . .
There it is—that haunting, mincing "but."
There is one I long for, desire; her ability, power
to make wrinkles disappear under pressure and heat.
She is stunning. Simply stunning.
Rowenta, I will have you. I will have you.

LEAVING BOB

Shock blinds her
when her father dies suddenly.
She's a racehorse kicking
through a haze of sorrow
packing toiletries and tears
in a small overnight bag.

Before her blue Dodge pick-up is saddled
with her dog and scant luggage
and before she makes the commute
from Texas to New Mexico,
she asks, "Would you check on Bob
a couple of times a day?"
He's a stray she picked up,
nursed for several years.

When I first meet my ward, he rejects me.
His bulky gray back arches with the power
of his lion cousins.
Copper eyes pin me with anger.
Arrow sharp claws stab at me
from the lap of a rocking chair
as he hisses with a primitive warrior's voice.

I breathe in fear while searching for a shield,
find a blanket folded on the corner of the couch.
I toss it over Bob as though it is a cotton net.
My hands shake while I pour his dried meal.
The kitchen counter and floor are pastures of panic
littered with dehydrated kernels.

I back towards the door; we stare at each other,
come to a truce. He retreats behind a chair
and I walk out into a cold wild stuttering wind,
shiver enough for the both of us

EARLY MORNING SYMPHONY

Those cardinals started their recital early this morning.
Light was barely a thought when I opened my eyes
to their performance.

The wind moved like a body with clumsy knees.
It bumped shrubs and the silk plants on my patio
as it moved up, down the sidewalk.

I didn't know the wind's destination,
but a medley of sounds trailed it—
dogs barking, doors slamming,
water rushing like Niagara
from the shower upstairs.

I gradually tuned out their recitations
as my mind straddled those moments
between wake and sleep.
I curled my body into the womb of a warm blanket,
drifted back to the place of dreams.

THE TRUTH BEHIND "ONCE UPON A TIME"

I'd like to drag everyone around me to happiness.
—Beverlye Hyman Fead

This poem is a fairy tale
of a woman, the stench of sleep
still on her breath, the smell of sweat
sticky on her skin after last night's hot flash.
She is unkempt this December morning.
The hair in the back of her head smashed
to the scalp and the remaining curly locks
shooting at a rented popcorn ceiling.
She does not shower yet, a protest
against last night's dream.
It is a recurring fable of her slumber.

A little girl, seven, with feral innocence,
models a new navy-blue and orange
polka-dot pleated dress, black shoes, white socks.
She thinks she is beautiful, a princess twirling
in the castle of light and air.
She hears only the clicking of her heels
against the sidewalk, not her aunt scolding,
He ain't paid me back for that dress yet.

A tiara of delight trembles on her head
as she rides the horse of his shoulders.
They gallop away from rejection—
that ancient boogey-man, into a slanted sunset.
She calls him Daddy; he answers with a smile.
They both kick against the blue stone of her birth.

IV. THROUGH THE SEASONS

We laughed and the world was light.
We laughed and the cool night air grew warm with joy.
We laughed and life was simple.

WHEN THE EARTH WRITES POETRY

She drafts West Texas
with its contradictions of tongues and heat,
potpourri of yellow-hand dawns
and orange-mouth dusks
yawning over desolate flatlands.

She doodles knots of tumbleweeds
outside the margins of skimpy-grass plains
after the failed revision of a mesquite's thorny arms.
She scribbles in long-hand the prickly pear,
pine oak forest, and juniper savannahs.

She hums the ambient drone of cicadas
and the weepy yaps of coyotes
while scrawling over the Guadalupe Mountains.
When caliginous light crawls
over *El Capitan's* rugged crest,
she stretches her back
and leans with the sharp of her elbows
into the boundaries of night.

When the sky, that ancient archivist,
opens dusky records of the heavens,
she sits on her wide rump
in her ruched dress of solitude.
Her hem drags across the desert
as she writes run-on sentences with the stars.

ON WEATHER

I'm neither goddess nor priestess,
but know the sermon of the earth
and weather's simple language.

There is no guile on its pure tongue,
and its skin is too transparent for deceit.
It does not covet the sky's reputation
nor envy shanties praising the sea.

It has no secrets to uncover
and no hidden desire to be anything
other than what it is.
See its power?
It changes constantly like a traffic signal
synchronized to its own whims.
How it makes humans puppets
by adjusting the sun's thermostat—
dress, undress, pray, complain
retreat, repent, rejoice?

Look at that half naked lady dancing in the doorway,
speaking into an indifferent night
hands fluttering like butterfly wings.
She says, "Beautiful is the sky's bushy black brows!
We have not seen them for over two hundred days."
The rain came like a celebrity, laughing with wet mischief
and tapping on windows with its soft knuckles—
neither a slave or indentured servant
to the meteorologists' predictions.

Am I immoral to long for such freedom,
to be jealous of the sun and rain?
They neither wear watches nor pencil occasions on calendars.
Their use for time is as purposeful as this circus of dried leaves
clogging that drainage ditch.
They are not tricked into believing what is now is always.

BANDANA SUNDAY

To find Odessa,
look where the wind blows above the 20 mph speed limit
and sand twirls like helicopter rotors.
Flying dirt feels like millions of tiny blades
cutting through skin and tooth enamel.
Trashcan lids flap like wild tongues.

My neighbor is masked in a blue bandana
piloting a lawnmower.
It rumbles louder than a chopper
as it shoots grassy clouds of dust.
His gaze is fixed straight ahead
looking through the cockpit of heat and sweat.
Avoiding rocks and thirsty roses,
he maneuvers the mower with the skill of a pilot.

I walk to my car and the air with its grainy hands
sandpapers my face, cracks my lips
and leaves welts of dryness on my tongue.
But my eyes water as I drive past him
wondering—what is the urgency with his lawn?
Why doesn't he wait until the sky tickets the wind,
slows it down and cuffs it into stillness?

SPRING THIRST

Those who dwell in the desert
know what it's like to be nails
beneath the sun hammering
one hundred ten degrees of fortitude.
It's the shade of grit that allows us to live
where the sky is a leaking ceiling
of dry heat.

Six months this earth cries with thirst,
begs to feel rain's wet fingers
digging in cracked and desolate places.
But rain keeps its hands hidden behind clouds,
forces us to survive on dew, wells, hoses,
and last year's showers.

Over weeks I watch drought return
my mother's lawn to dirt—
back to its beginnings before seed or man.
Throughout the block, emerald green blades fade pale
like blond straw, bush limbs are lemon colored
and my neighbor's morning glories sag with humility.

I kneel, the weight of sweat heavy
on my shoulders, pruning, pulling
weeds while the sun bruises my back
with its hot pounding,
daring me to take a drink.

WATERING THE GARDEN

When death comes like the hungry bear in autumn...
I was hurrying through my own soul,
opening its dark doors—I was leaning out; I was listening...
—Mary Oliver

Miss Mary Oliver, I read "Violets"
before watering this morning.
I should like to meet you
down by the rumbling creek and the tall trees;
you can show me the place of your violet-scented past.

Come home with me, see the small space
where I planted a life garden.
The mound around the periwinkles looks like a fresh grave;
death is fresh in my life.

It did not *come like the hungry bear in autumn.*
It came in January, the desert was shedding
cold dry air like old snake skin.

You can see how my sunflowers,
marigolds, zinnias, daisies
hang limp—heavy with water,
the earth beneath their rod like legs
drinking greedily, but with thanksgiving.
Isn't it curious how most living things thirst?

More curious still, when *you were hurrying*
through your own soul, opening its dark doors—
leaning out, listening;
I was offering smiles to a robin and my neighbor
while pruning leaves, pulling grass and weeds;
she walked away, taking my smile with her.

The robin hung around long enough to watch
the sun shift its weight—
heat rushing from its large yellow feet.

FLOOD

The library's artificial air is a clumsy monkey.
Its cool hands slip away from the hem of my ankle-pants
as I walk into the afternoon, play a game of chicken
with the humidity speeding towards my face.
I retreat in to the cave of my car
where the aroma of leftover fusty pizza sits on the floor.

The lyrics of *Sincerely* are still rolling off my tongue
as I pull in the driveway and gather up the frayed
end of a grocery bag filled with four audio books.
I walk inside my home with words compressed in plastic.

Above the roof, charcoal clouds apron the sky
and outside my window, a festival of colors—
geraniums with flirtatious red smiles,
begonias with pursed pink painted lips,
sunflowers with dribbling yellow hair,
and purple fingered morning glories
crawling through twines of green.

I toss the bag on the couch, humming *Sincerely*,
as water gushes out of the darkened clouds
as though Moses just lifted his rod and struck the rock.

BRUISED

Two weeks ago this desert West Texas town
languished, watched a bullying sun
train orange knuckles on the city.
It jabbed air—skin with temperatures
of one hundred degrees and more.
Light was hot; dust was hot; boredom was hot.

Patches of bruised yellow grass,
garden plants streaked with heat welts,
city utility workers' sweat-stained uniforms
were proof of brutal beating.
The wind, too lazy or scared to help,
wouldn't even lift its hands to blow hair.

This afternoon, when I tried to nap,
that fickle wind howled, complained,
flailed its arms at a graying sky.
Windows, wind-chimes, trees trembled at its tirade.

A cavalry of heavy clouds, decked in black hats
strolled in from the east, covered the city.
Wind cowed into stillness and the sun
rolled down its sleeves in defeat.
I slept, the air a sponge of cool relief.
Rain—a wet gauze of healing.

AT THE SAN ANGELO SYMPHONY JULY 3RD
POPS CONCERT ON THE CONCHO RIVER

The sky is a black canteen.
Stars dribble from the flask of darkness
like a leaky faucet over flocks
of people perched in front of the River Stage
at the San Angelo Symphony July 3rd Pops Concert.

The battle between drought and the Southwest
is longer than the Battle of Verdun.
Tonight patriotic songs rain from the orchestra,
shower the audience with
America, A Salute to the Arm Forces,
Stars and Stripes Forever.

Before the full storm of melodies,
we stand soaking in sweat, silence, reverence
as *The Star-Spangled Banner* wets patriotism.
A parade of white gloved soldiers
stand at attention;
their faces are drenched in discipline.
A retired marine's eyes water,
his cheeks are pools of tears.
Can he see his comrades
marching across his memories?

Children's voices are canons of mirth
when red, orange, green, and blue fireworks
explode and shrapnel of light swim
through space like tadpoles.

And when the air swallows the last crack of a skyrocket
and note of celebration, we walk away,
leave the Concho River humming with white fire.

OF DEAD BEGONIAS

July's dusty throat is sore with drought.
The city has not known rain since November.

She is a patriot of planting, sprays a plot of earth
hotter than Lucifer's tongue every Wednesday and Sunday
with the fortitude of weeds. Water restrictions
make the other five days forbidden like Eve's apple.

There is only a fistful of zinnias
living out of a litter of three packages.
Moonflowers thrive but she wants more—
the sunflowers' full buttery heads,
the marigolds' mahogany puffy noses,
and the morning glories' strong skinny arms
snaking up her trellises, fence and walls
with fingers of pale blue and shocking lilac.

Out of desperation or love,
she lets the hose run when Friday cloaks
itself with a black cape.
Even with this, there is no redemption
for her beloved flowers.

Saturday evening she drops to her knees, postured
for absolution. Her wet sin was for naught.
 Her brow moistens with resignation.
With naked hands, she pulls dead begonias
and buries them in a black plastic bag.
Their brown withered heads the coda
of a hymn with two hundred days of dry verses.

LIQUID FISTS

This is West Texas where dry August heat clogs air
like excessive lint in a dryer chute.
It's raining. It rained yesterday and the day before.
This is rare as a blue moonstone.

I fall asleep with lightning blinking
through the blinds like a shorted light switch.
This morning I wake to the scent of fresh moisture
pooling in front of my door.

Last night's rain became heavy
liquid fists pounding the city.
Continuous beating did not bruise,
but healed dried yellow patches of earth.

The greedy famished ground
stores wetness like a last supper.
Overhead, a rainbow arches in the sky—
a period at the end of a long wet sentence.

RETURN

November's back from holiday
after trekking for twelve months across
the glossy white roads of the calendar.

Its primal instinct is to arrive without much fanfare,
but look at it this morning with its wide blue smile
and one big tooth hanging with polished grace.

The wind-brushed trees are swept
into bad comb-overs. Baldness is prevalent
in an assortment of them primping around the city.
What confidence to stand in such fullness—
as though the bushy green afros that started growing
in the spring were still hanging over their strong branches.

Oaks, ashes and birches know there is beauty in bareness,
honesty in revealing the skeleton of strength.
Each autumn, without protest,
they allow the elements
 to strip them of their leaves.
What if the soul was deciduous,
permitted life to remove those superficial coverings
that prevent us from seeing the true gifts in others?

With cold draped over its generous arm,
and Thanksgiving in its busy hand cutting
through sheets of love like a hungry pair of scissors,
November's back, crafting paper dolls out of gratitude.

STUCK IN THE GRAY

A Mr. Blue Northerner came trundling
in like some 1950's tough cowboy,
his holster loaded with two cans of spray paint—
gray and white. He was not satisfied
with his fancy antics of coat tugging
and head bending moves.
He clogged traffic from street to sky.
Denver's steel birds are nesting
in a soft ivory wall.

Christmas is next Monday
and I am in Chicago where Mr. Blue
is holding the city hostage.
I want to go home
where the air is a warm cotton sweater
and the earth's feet are comfortable
in brown desert shoes.

I lean against my hotel window
press into the oppression
of this Northern thug
and watch a hard cold stream of tears explode
from the skies. Pop! Pop! Pop!
Drops are wet bullets ricocheting from tops
of black umbrellas racing up and down Michigan Avenue.

Darkness gallops in, wrestles with Mr. Blue
and pins his harassing arms behind his back.
The crying stops. The bullying stops.
And rain is a whisper behind its dull black armor.

OPENING DRAWERS

Maybe haste is the nimble-fingered juggler
snatching scarves as I pull them out of the drawer.
A kaleidoscope of fabrics leap through the air
then pile on my bed. The soft colors press together
the way words do in closed books.
Not here.

I open a sister drawer, see a squint of silver
wedged in the corner. A necklace has slipped
from its pouch the way the first moment of morning does
when the desire to sleep is stronger than the desire to wake.
Did haste clumsily draw the mouth shut?
Is this how it slipped into the light? No matter.
Not there.

I stretch the necklace to its full length, leave it on the dresser,
search one more drawer, find a hodgepodge of treasures—
a Cross pen/pencil set, penny passports, a silver charm bracelet
and other things the oak bottom and I will keep to ourselves.

Curious how opening drawers is like opening life,
finding beautiful trinkets of pleasure while searching
for the bland amulet of need.

With urgency nagging at me and the clock gnawing my heels,
I wrap a brown wool scarf around my neck,
grab the matching coat and feel a bulge in one pocket.
My gloves!

How glorious to find protection after preparing to walk
into the world with bare knuckles, bracing myself
for a frigid winter handshake.

BARE

This morning my poem went skinny dipping.
Ripped those garments of alliteration, assonance, metaphors
and left them in a pile along the window ledge.

I thought its desire to be an exhibitionist,
show off the skin of its form
was a taunt, a ruse to insight me to redress it.

But it was sweating boredom
after continuously repeating:
For eight months the sky has worn
the same itchy blue boa of dehydration.
The sun clawed into the flesh of day
until the air was raw with heat.

There was no guile in the poem,
too many layers of marigolds, zinnias and roses.
Before leaping from the page,
it shouted, "It's dry and hot.
Let me jump bare into a cold pond of simplicity."

V. SCARRED TEMPLE

TRAIN RIDE

I am riding a train I never purchased a ticket for.
I try to get off every time it stops at a station,
but the door is locked;
I can't get off and no one can get on.
At each stop there is always a hand
pointing forward.

A SUDDEN DARKNESS

I was huddled in the last stall
in the bathroom at work
with my heart trying to tear through my flesh.
I became a beetle caged in blackness
when darkness descended with no warning.
My legs searched my memory,
hoping to quickly learn how to move.
I used my hands for eyes, jutted them out
before me, felt along the wall;
my bridge to light?
To somewhere other than the prison
where my breath was locked
behind the bars of my ribs.
I reached the sink, turned on the water
and let the stream dribble through my fingers.

Curious how rituals follow us even in the cave of panic,
the washing of hands, the crossing of fingers, prayer.

Last night I prayed for winter to come
brush me with its sharp cold bristles,
dig in my scalp of heat, freeze the flashes
of misery that come abruptly
when cancer takes you as wife.

Oh, when cancer took me as wife
I mothered sadness with her pouty curls
and long heavy skirt,
fear with her jaundice laugh
and choleric cry.
I tell this husband of darkness

I don't care how strong my thighs,
do not ask me to birth
anything more
than what I am carrying
in this swollen painful minute.

AT THE TABLE

. . . and shines against the hard possibility
—Mary Oliver

Cancer, gluttonous deviant,
will eat through your soul,
that shapeless sister
who lives beneath the skin,
if you let it. I did.

Who can truly shine
against the hard possibility of death
without fear, that club-foot giant?
It trudges in the caverns of my mind.
pounding against the deep abyss of my faith.

I wonder if the children across the Indian Ocean
can hear my fear, too? Or are the bombs and guns
growling like a starving stomach too loud?
Love, you magician, let your belly swell
with hunger quickly!
War, that two-fisted bully,
is more insatiable than cancer.
It digs sharp teeth into those who cannot tie their shoes
while vendors of power sit at the table
with a place they claim to reserve for peace.

What face does peace have?
Is it a bearded man or wrinkled woman?
Does it have long fingers and short stubby toes?
What of its mouth? Does it have full lips?
Thin pink ones? Perky dimples?

What if it has the smooth countenance of innocence?

Can we trust it will break bread, drink wine with us?
Or will betrayal dissolve itself into a water glass?
It slithered its way into the supper of Jesus
and his community of twelve.

Curious how the things we weigh and measure—
silver, a strip of land, a bowl of fruit—
dictate our purpose.

Loneliness crowds into the chair across from me
as I bypass the fruit bowl, eat a plush spinach dip
and watch reruns of The Property Brothers.
A sudden explosion of heat bursts in my body.
I open a window. The last light of this sleepy day
is draining into the deep cup of history.
I invite the cold wind to perform a tarantella
on my window ledge as night
stretches a gray tablecloth across the sky.

MONDAY MAMMOGRAM: A CONVERSATION WITH KARLA K.

Let us stand back to back fighting this disease—
fist curled raised to our faces—
And though life is that bull that doesn't want to be ridden,
Let us ride him anyway.
—Karla K. Morton

Anxiety chews through minutes
while I sit in a small rectangular room
waiting for the moment a cold steel mouth
will clutch its plastic tooth on the soft swells of my life.

You've sat waiting like this, too—
flipping through magazines, eyes scanning
models with glossy expressions and hair
more brilliant than the waiting room's lights.

Days pass. An envelope with the hospital's name
embossed on the left corner is deposited
in my mailbox. It is a lone carrier pigeon
with the mammogram results.
I read, toss the news aside, walk into the day
ticking off errands I must run.

But you had no carrier pigeon like this;
your news traveled through thin wires
where a small word sounded like an earthquake!
You said, *The mammogram was Tuesday.*
The biopsy, Wednesday. I got the call Thursday
and cancer stepped onto my front porch and rang the doorbell.

What power—the way you answered
that intrusive solicitor! You showed it how

beauty is redefined in perseverance, street savvy,
and the beefed-up, flexing muscles of the soul.
When you (and others) met cancer at the door,
the color of courage and might changed.
Strength is now a pair of pink boxing gloves.
You have sparred with radiation, chemo and mastectomies
while fear punched your beautiful bodies with blows
that could not keep you down. I will fight this disease
with you sisters. But for now, I uncurl my raised fist
to lovingly massage the bruised and tender places in your spirits.

*Note: All italicized words are from Karla K. Morton's book "Redefining
Beauty."*

CHEMO: DAY THREE

Pluck one strawberry.
Eat it because you can today.
When that third day jab flattens you
and water feels like cotton clogging
your throat, nausea is bare fists
throwing hooks and right crosses
in the pit of your stomach
and you curl into the ropes
of your bed waiting
for the referee of sleep to call the fight,
you will want this moment
with its red stained fingers
and pitted jaws.

HOW TO FIGHT LIKE A GIRL

To fight like a girl
you must first become an ocean
to hold the crush of tears
pooling beneath the ducts.

You must learn to walk
through the day with a fish of fear
floating through
the coral of your belly.

At the sound of battle,
you must paint your nails
the boldest blood shade of red
and use them like shark teeth
to maim and masticate
those piranha emotions
gnawing at your strength.

You must get off your knees
after the tentacles of cancer and chemo,
nausea and fatigue, pain and weakness
grasp your body and feed on all things woman.

You must remember you are a woman
when lavas of sweat roll from your bald head
and flank your face, and your lips crack and flake
like a dried beach.

You must stand straight, wash yourself in softness,
tattoo stars on your fists and sing praises
for the half-moons in the sky of your breasts.

MONOLOGUE OF A PAPER TOWEL

Fat quiet hovers around the ceiling,
the meat of sound gone home with the children.
With pad, pen and book, she heads out
to job number two at the Texas Oncology Center.
It is work to sit in *the chair*,
balance small talk, sleep, and words.
Her mind, that bulldozer, pushes back tears,
packs them in the bowls of her eyelids.
But with two strong breaths
the concrete of her resolve can crack,
send wet tracks down the avenue of her cheeks.
Her body switches professions;
the skin above her heart a pincushion—
needles drive a line into the port stitched in her vein.
With eyes gripped shut, she collects other people's years
like paychecks—twenty, ten, five years free
while machines chit-chat and drip poison
from their small plastic mouths into her.
Not crying is her new vocation
and sweat is a disease spreading on her clothes;
she uses me like a tongue
to lick her overnight condition,
squeezes me as though cancer is a spill
she can wipe away.

SEPTEMBER THIRTEENTH

For Javin Contreras

The mastectomy is penciled in like charcoal on glass
for September thirteenth. Fate changes shoes, goads my destiny
with its sharp stick; I take a detour. Instead of dressing incisions
made by the surgeon's knife, I am listening
to the buzz and whir, feeling the teeth of the hairdresser's clippers
mowing through my thick black hair.
I counted the first two gray strains that webbed my temples;
then I stopped. Hair, like stars and sand, clouds and grass
was not created for the count, rather for the dalliance of the wind.
Flickers of tears mingle with water and shampoo
as the beautician massages my head. Her fingers move
over the scroll of my scalp as though she is reading Braille.
The two friends who accompany me tell my how elegant
and in vogue I look with short hair. But at that moment,
their words are not strong enough to dam the tears.

September Fourteenth
I go to school with my head covered
by a blue scarf lined with a canopy of white stars,
knotted and tied with shame.
Students question me with their eyes. No answer.

September Fifteenth
I find the strength to wear my shaved head to a restaurant.
Javin dressed in his eleven-year-old coat of courage
comes to tell me, *Miss Walker you shouldn't cover your head.*
You look beautiful.
He will sing a solo in the Christmas pageant.
Not because he says I am beautiful,
but because his voice is beautiful.

Now
I wear red lipstick and crimson polish
to cover my chemo shadowed nails.
My bald head longs for the chopped black locks.
I only have a handful stashed in a bronze box
growing into memories.

WHEN I WAS IN SAN FRANCISCO

and the dust returns to the ground it came from
and the spirit returns to God who gave it.
Ecclesiastes 12:7

My anger was not a pile of red bricks
and cancer was not eating into my happiness.
I was like a seagull dandling inland;
I dared not to venture beyond the sandy mat
where the Pacific did backward somersaults.
But I did go to the edge of that ocean,
snapped a picture of a mermaid
someone crafted on the beach.
I named her Mystery and wondered
if she would return to shapeless dust
before the moon washed over her tail.
I did not see the creator
who drug his chilly hands through damp sand,
drew an outline of myths and legends
while his lungs filled with salty air.
And I did not see him walk away with her
gritty essence floating underneath his fingernails.

SLEEPING HOT

My modesty is a mare
galloping across moist sheets.
Heat and water pour from my pores
as though the bed is a trough.
My hands move like wild hooves
kicking off nightcap, T-shirt, pajama bottoms
and all things cotton.
My bare body hugs the headboard,
hoping the cool oak will chill my hot flesh.
I remember rain for the morning.
I want it to do a ballet over my body
like a masseuse's fingers
kneading knots and stretching muscles.
Or gracefully bathe me with its wet beauty
like a hula dancer's hypnotic hips
and artful hands writing the message
of her ancestors.

DAWSON, TEXAS 1958

The sweaty salty smell of birth pressed against the walls
of the small house in Dawson, Texas.
It was September but an exhausted summer kept kicking out heat.
The sky above the piney woods murmured with a mouthful of stars
and yawned exposing a long black tongue of darkness.
A child wailed her way into the world, testing her voice in light and
air,
arms and legs flailing, reaching as though night was her father.

Did the stars in their ancient wisdom know
that in fifty five years she would be exiled
to a leather chair with *the red devil*
dripping in her veins? That the devil would return her
body to baldness even as it was at birth?
With her eyes closed in prayer, she receives the wind's covenant.
She listens to the holiness of its fanfare
trumpeting in the castle of her skin.

JOY ON THE HEELS OF BROKENNESS

For joy is a great romping beast straining to be tackled...
— June Rachuy Brindel

Wednesday is an equator dividing the work week
into hemispheres of tolerance.
I choose this day to unveil the mystery and sadness
buried beneath my cache of hats and scarves.
An axis of anticipation spins in my music classroom;
for weeks students beg, "Let us see."
Their eyes are lanterns shimmering
in the dark tent of my dread.
With a trembling hand, I reach
towards months of vulnerability.
I slide a black beret from my head
onto my first two fingers, use them like a hat rack
and use the beret as a shield,
but exposure is the only covering
draped over my predominately bald head.
A sparse grove of gray shades the area above my ears;
soft curly strands are scattered like fallen leaves.

My spirit is an egg; I feel fear crack
it while probing the students' faces.
There is no measure of silence.
Their response sounds rehearsed,
orchestrated by fate when they shriek in unison,
"You have white hair!"
Maybe baldness to six year olds is a spotless
water glass filled with light
because the disappointment in not seeing only skin
is thicker than banana pudding.

We distance ourselves from the unveiling,
spend the morning singing songs that require smiles.
Sadness is a predator, but life has a way of baiting and trapping
it in a cage of joy.

WHAT CANCER SOUNDS LIKE

This is for the welder who added another concrete step
to the stairs outside an apartment.
The flames of his drill scorched a new coat of pale green paint.

It is for the mail carrier who sorted through lives
folded and fitted into slivers of white bark.
He stuffed stern warnings, cheerful hellos,
pleading goodbyes into small metal boxes
as a box fan whirled air around his hairy ankles.

It is for those who waited at a bus stop
watching motorists revel in the cold air
streaming from car vents
while heat stepped on their toes.

It is for the truck driver who listened
to his left turn signal blink in two/four meter
as he tapped his rough hands on the steering wheel.

It is for the lady who the welder apologized to for making noise,
who opened the letter left in her box—
Results of your exam indicate an abnormal area. . .

When the doctor said, *You have cancer*, she remained silent
as she listened to inverted screams echo in her lungs;
they were too loud to pass through her vocal chords.

EXAMINATIONS STORIES

July is on a ten-speed bicycle
riding fast, riding high up the hill to August.
But the marathon starts in June
when Dr. One probes for a lump;
his hands find only a flat surface.

June falls behind, a flat tire in this race.
Sometime between these months a mass
rises like bread, and on Independence Day
my fingers brush across the sore angry bump.

I call Dr. One. He says, *You need a mammogram.*
The technician and I talk about her daughter's future
plans while she presses my breast between the cold mouth
of the x-ray machine. *We need to do a sonogram.*
She takes me to another room, leaves me stretched
on the table, her face a scroll of fear.
Dr. Two enters the room, examines the screen, tells the tech
It is not a cyst. Tells me, *Your doctor will get in touch.*

The nurse from Dr. One's office calls and asks,
What kind of surgeon do you want? Male or female?
She rolls off a litany of surgeons. I chose one,
give Dr. Three a call. July is riding fast up the hill
when Dr. Three says, *You have cancer.*
She gives me the number for Dr. Four.
He orders CT and bone scans.
What other mysteries will they reveal?
Another lump? Lesion? Lone tear lodged in the kidney?
Drink lots of water.
Will it flood this leech, cancer, camped in my breast?
Or change the direction of these painted palm trees
in examination room number two?

A voice will tell you when to hold your breath.
When the technician walks away with her lab coat tapping
against her confident thighs and closes the door,
I forget to wait for the command, take a deep breath.
I gasp the stillness crawling in the room,
tune into the synchronized hum of machine,
my rumbling heart, footsteps abandoning me
to breathe in the sanctuary of cold white loneliness.

WATCHING FROM THE CHAIR BY THE WINDOW

We start this dance of fear in July
when the sun is building pyramids of heat.
Thursday, that limbo day we flatten our backs
without shimmying our way to the weekend.
Anxiety, a pair of bongo drums we beat
on the way to West Texas Oncology Center.

My stomach flinches, the nurse gloves up in latex,
connects the IV lines.
Chemo's cold ravages me from the inside.
Carol tucks a brown blanket beneath my feet,
plugs in the heating pad, sits in the chair by the window
where a seamless stream of light cascades.
We chat, place a bet on how long
it will take me to fall prey to sleep.
This is our ritual for a trinity of seasons,
lab work, doctors' appointments, chemo sessions.

From our window chairs,
we spend a myriad of Thursdays scrutinizing the sky.
October, we witness it cry apologetically all afternoon.
Its dull beam floods the day with wet sympathy.
January, we watch it explode with white.
Tiny crystal shards stick to streets, buildings, bald trees.
March, a blush of warmth fills its wide face.
A drowsy smile is edged in the angles of my mouth.
Carol wakes me from a Benadryl induced sleep,
snaps pictures of me with nurses and bobbing balloons.

Time burns through seconds
until they are heaped into a rubble of centuries.
We've been friends for less, but know how years
leap into that incessant flame.

HOMECOMING

Mom, I am glad her hair has grown back,
and I like that silver in it. —Beckett Baer

Spring, heat scrapes against winter's cold shoulders.
Temperatures clash—
low forties in the a.m., high seventies in the p.m.

A lone white coil springs
from the crown of my scalp.
I smile a hyena's grin,
brush my fingers across to make it bounce.
My head has not known sun, wind,
hair since last September.
Chemo consumed it, left a sheen of baldness.
I covered it with the soft folds of scarves
and fancy brimmed hats.
I forgot the way locks felt between my fingers
when I braided the thick ebony strains,
or slicked it back to flaunt a faux bun
on the nape of my neck.

October, a commune of curls
encroaches on the once barren landscape of my head.
Gray, once an interloper,
weaves itself throughout the vast blackness
growing its way back home.

VI. SHUTTING THE DOORS

On the other side of her dream, she sees the light of joy,
and a moth beating its powdery gray life
in the basket of a child's palms.

THE SCREAM

After viewing Edvard Munch's
Der Schrei der Natur (The Scream of Nature)

If you let go of your Halloween
peanut-candy corn-coated breath,
it will become a ghost in the city of Odessa.
Not like that cheery chubby Casper cartoon
or those grotesque movie ghouls—
rather, a spirit of relief floating in an October chill.
Is this how we make the world small?
Through breath and air?
Maybe the redwoods in California
will smell the sweet aroma of your release.

If you dress yourself in a coat of curiosity
while driving around these overcrowded concrete streets,
you will see the city's dress is summer green
with a hem of frightened yellow, drab brown
and a collar of panicked orange.
Munch mimics fall with the same hues
in *Der Schrei der Natur.*
The contorted face he sketched
in his whirlwind of colors
is no more terrifying than my dreams
rummaging through the darkness, fishing for stars.
Is this what fear looks like,
a distorted jaw and murky shadows?
If so, does a violet scream joy?

If we wait until tomorrow to remove our masks,
truth will follow us into November.
You will see beneath this flesh I am a pole.
Your words lean against everything you once feared.

THE DISSEMINATION OF GREEN

It isn't so much that you are unraveling the mystery,
as much as the mystery is unraveling you.
—Disembodied Poetics

Time had no pulse.
All the earth was green
and there was no color difference between
flesh of fowl, flesh of flower, flesh of foe.

The Southern sky said to its emerald clouds,
"Your tongue shall not taste nor touch
the mouths of those in the North.
The layers of their lips are too flat
and inferior to our heft."

The Northern sky said to its jade clouds,
"Your hands shall not embrace nor stroke
the puffy faces of those in the South.
The bulbous cheeks are inferior to our sleekness."

The Western sky said to its myrtle clouds,
"Your fingers shall not massage nor braid
the curly heads of those in the East.
The twisted locks are inferior to our smoothness."

Fever filled with combs of orange flame
scratched through brush,
left scars of red barren dried land.

A scream ripped through the clouds.
The sound was filled with such fear the skies paled
into a faint shade of blue.
The clouds tried to flee, but became enmeshed.

Their soft bodies became dark with confusion.
Their tears streaked all living creatures below.
When the crying stopped, all of the clouds were drained.
Their green skin became white with release,
their sore throats were silenced.

The earth was wet with color
and creation blushed
with a kaleidoscope of differences.
The peacock with its feathery back
embraced the Maypop with its purple veins.
And so it was with all living things.
Then from the edge of the earth,
in the midst of the chorus of harmony
a thin voice cried,

"Who am I?"

The wind answered in passing,
"You are mystery.
A jittery gold leaf trapped
between stone and sun."

METHUSELAH'S CURSE

*Methuselah is the world's oldest individual tree. (4,765 years). It lives
10,000 feet above sea level in the Inyo National Forest, California. The
tree is hidden in a grove called the Forest of Ancients.
To protect the tree from vandalism, the forest service keeps its exact
location secret—Wired Science*

Does rain have a soul?
Understand the hunch of shoulders
beneath its touch
or body so grateful in its embrace
the stomach aches with joy?

I know the mockingbird has a song,
a sharp sacred hymn of contentment.
It sings all afternoon
a tribute to the wind's slow wave
and a Corgi's lazy sniff.

And Methuselah in his ancient brown vest,
rough dusty trunk and lonely twisted limbs
sits in solitude not of his making.

Wonder if they let him smell chocolate's decadence,
taste a watermelon's red sweet stickiness
feel the soft stomach of a slice of bread,
interviewed him before tucking him away?
He knows history's secret—
that it slows us down, anchors us
in the easy chairs of the past.

But he doesn't know the stroke of a hand,
the brush of elbow, the caress of a child.

He thrives in the hostile desert,
a hood of seclusion veils his gnarled life—
his ancient body a marquee for loneliness.

TO A BROKE POET

There's not much difference between star and stone
in the hard sky of need. Stones can be dealt,
but who can shuffle or cut a star?
Can the fat tail of a comet fill an empty stomach
or even odds? Ask the broke poet
who tries to stuff the Milky Way in the cup
of her obsession; she is driven by need to tempt the decks.
This image junky stares at the moon,
sees an eye bulging from the socket of night,
depends on words and constellations for her fix.

She reads messages in the wind, swears
the breeze bru—shhhh, brush, brushing against the window
is the sharp elbow of the earth
prodding, prompting her to bet everything
she doesn't own. Love or luck makes her believe
air and the plump voices of morning
are hers to wager.

Once she slid an ace of diamonds
in the ribs of her poems, then sat at the blackjack table.
Her face was as intimidating as a blank sheet of paper.
She stacked metaphors like poker chips,
dared the dealer to challenge them.
She tapped the table with her BIC's
as though the odds were in the pen.
Hit me. *Again. Again. Again.*
When the last card busted her hand,
she dropped the ace on the stack,
broke into a smile then walked away humming
with the breeze bru—shhhh, brush, brushing against the window.

DISSERTATION OF A CHAIR

There is no wisdom in throwing pepper
into a dizzy wind,
trying to handcuff time
to the rusty hinges of an old refrigerator door,
using a grease-caked spoon to carve your name
or saying we are all alike—
even if we all are the color of an orange
and have matching hairy backs
and floppy bottoms that open and shut like a trashcan lid.
I am *Center Aisle E-109* and know the weight
of the man with the wolf beard and the word *Wrangler*
crowded in the seams of his worn faded jeans.
His purple shirt struggles to stay tucked
as music swarms around his stomach—
sagging like a sack of stones
and the desire to dance gallops across his booted feet.

Center Aisle A-122 tries to restrain a woman
with laughter leaking from the smooth
corners of her mouth.
The black sweater tattooed on her torso
is a testament she's accustom to the hypnotic response
of men; their eyes freeze on her gyrating pendulum.
Her tiny hips are deft as she wiggles rhythms of seduction.
The sharpened aroma of Budweiser and cheese
on her breath is a predator surrounding the gray-haired
couple dressed in matching retro Jimi Hendrix T-shirts.
They sit close enough to tangle their mirth with hers.

Who can know the lady leaning against the wall is lonely?
Her head bobs as she listens to a blend of Blues
and contaminated voices; there is no distinction

between female and male as excitement spreads
from seat to seat.

The Gray One knows.
Her white blouse and black slacks are stained with longing;
she wishes her mother was here.

But she's miles away from her daughter's yearning,
stacking the routine of clothes across her chair's soft back,
resting her metal legs against one of its steel wheels.
In the morning, steel and metal will carry her
to that place where she dances with dialysis.
Here—the lights flush out darkness
while the lonely one watches people spill
under a sky where darkness is damming the light.
I am writing about a spoon smuggled beneath my bottom,
how its slick silver tongue has tasted the world in all of its
differences.

SILENCED

Perhaps it's stuttering rain against the window, the wet
hymn of hope singing in the chorus of a strong wind,

or maybe it's the small head of a morning glory
peeking through dirt burdened with three years of drought,

or it could be the soft words that have a way of burrowing
through bone and walls we build with past injuries

to reach that one we do not want to lose

that makes me believe I can pump peace
into the violent, bloodlust veins

of nations wanting to rule by silencing the tongue.

OUT OF THE DARKNESS

      ‿orn sliver of red defiance
   ‿igs outside this hotel window.
If the moon had hands,
it would brush the crimson nuisance,
this scarlet loiterer, from its cratered chin.
Brushing the city with lazy eyes,
I watch a rambling stream of car lights
with ruby glassy tails roll
into their unassuming lives.
How are they to know I am hovering here,
staring and leaving fingerprints on the slick pane?

I feel omnipotent in this spot.
If I stretch my arms, make them long
as the darkness, I can reach the bottom
of the penthouse suite; it's a floor above
this luscious room that is not mine.
And if I strain my imagination
against the television screen, I can hear
fireplaces on the East coast protesting
against this last storm.
The pop and crackle of flames plead
for winter's rampage to end.
Wet carnage from the sky is piled
three feet high at the foot of frigid houses.
Wonder why there are no caps for their sloped heads
or coats for their boxy bodies?
Claws of ice grip every big boned
bare branch in the tree family
and snow makes white arctic monasteries
out of reluctant cities.

When I try to imagine their cold,
sleep whistles at me from somewhere
between my heavy feet and throbbing shoulders.
I walk out into the long darkness
listening to sleep's soft tune while red
paints a self-portrait on the irises of my eyes.

A POET SHOULD NEVER TELL A PRIEST

That she feels like a goddess
when creating a universe out of a white void.
The black ink of her hands pens clay words,
shapes them genderless, forms a poem
from the ribs of syntax, memory,
and that box of marbles she calls life.

Autumn is on its knees crawling
towards the air, maples, the poet's bald head.
It wraps cool arms around the morning
as though begging forgiveness for three months
of brutal heat and Poet's chemotherapy.

Some prayers are lost beneath the wheels
of school busses bumping along back roads
in a desert West Texas town—
the screeching of their brakes are masked screams
of the abused earth and tired poet.

Anger is a string
of expletives beaded together;
it has no allegiance to any soul,
will wrap itself around
any raw exposed neck,
including the godly.

Night is a hotdog.
Stars dribble and multiply
over its long darkness
like mustard seeds.

LISTENING TO THE PAST

Her ears are horns blasting recognition.
Her head is a speaker she tilts in your direction,
leaning as though you can hear the fanfare
of your voice vibrating on her eardrum.
She smiles. You smile
at her like you did fifty years ago
when you think you hear
that one syllable that says who you are.

But it's not your name;
she hums the first bars
of your favorite song.
You swallow as though the melody is the meat of a fresh peach
and you listen as she hums her way back
to the one seat concert you can never attend.

AT SUNSET MEMORIAL FUNERAL HOME

I am not going to do a moral striptease.
—Nicole C. Mullen

The sun painted a huge smile across the sky
and we are in coats, chills tugging at our tails.
Sun where is your heat, honesty where are your shoes?
And how are we to wear our true selves
without stripping away the clothes of expectation
others have dressed us in?
And why does unveiling a flawed character
make others shiver?

How are we to cross this gulf
between morality and judgment?
Confession and sharing? Warning and wisdom?
Ponte di Rialto has its wooden pilings,
Landwasser its curvy limestone,
Mackinac its blue and white steely arm,
and life this pencil of time.
Curious how it resculptures the face,
draws lines of wisdom and folly beneath the brow.
We are born with breaths piled in us
like a five hundred count bag of cotton balls.

And when the bag is empty?
I am at Sunset Memorial Funeral Home
making my eyes like dams,
refusing to let tears roll over my lashes,
staring at the neon Jaguar Gold Club sign
across the street and wondering—
is death dancing, shedding pieces of sorrow
while gentlemen cackle at bare thighs?

POET DREAMING

No sky could hold so much light.
—Mary Oliver

Poems are nomads paddling through darkness
collecting words from the arms
of Orion, Sagittarius, and Perseus
before camping in a poet's dream.
She sees souls as colliding galaxies,
holes of light burning
with millions to trillions of stars
too bright to fit in the cavity of sky.

Those stars are poems
crammed in the dusty envelopes of mortal bodies,
shimmering beneath white ribbons of bone.
A silhouette of stars floats in the window of her eye.
The energy of need forces tiny hands to brush
against the small wings of a sigh hovering in the evening.

She hears the silhouette speak
in a voice the timbre of a piccolo,
"Look Mommy! I caught a butterfly."
On the other side of her dream, she sees the light of joy,
and a moth beating its powdery gray life
in the basket of a child's palms.

About the Author

Loretta Diane Walker teaches music at Reagan Elementary in Odessa, Texas. She graduated from Ector High School, received a Bachelor of Music Education degree from Texas Tech University and earned a Master's of Elementary Education from the University of Texas at the Permian Basin. Loretta is active in her community through membership in organizations such as, Delta Sigma Theta Sorority, Inc. and the Permian Basin Poetry Society. She is also a member of the Texas Music Educators Association, the Poetry Society of Texas, the Pennsylvania Poetry Society, Texas Mountain Trail Writers, the National Federation of State Poetry Societies, and serves as a volunteer at the Wagner Noel Performing Arts Center.

Loretta is a multiple Pushcart Prize Nominee. Her poems and essays appear in publications throughout the United States, Canada, and the UK. Her book *Word Ghetto* won the 2011 Blue Light Press Book Award. Miss Walker was elected as the 2014 "Community Statesman in the Arts" by the Heritage of Odessa Foundation.

CPSIA information can be obtained
at www.ICGtesting.com
Printed in the USA
FFOW02n1605080618
47064050-49442FF